Lyrics

Pathetic & humorous

from A to Z

by Edmund Dulac

Dover Publications, Inc.
Mineola, New York

Bibliographical Note

This Dover edition, first published in 2009, is an unabridged republication of the work originally published by Frederick Warne & Co., London and New York, 1908.

Library of Congress Cataloging-in-Publication Data

Dulac, Edmund, 1882–1953.
    Lyrics, pathetic & humorous from A to Z / Edmund Dulac.
        p. cm.
    Originally published: London ; New York : F. Warne & Co., 1908.
    ISBN-13: 978-0-486-47373-4
    ISBN-10: 0-486-47373-2
     1. Limericks. I. Title.

PR6007.U46L9 2009
821'.912—dc22

                                                  2009018988

Manufactured in the United States by Courier Corporation
47373201
www.doverpublications.com

Lyrics

Pathetic & humorous

A was an Afghan Ameer
Who played the accordion by ear.
When ambassadors called,
They first listened appalled,
Then would suddenly all disappear.

B was a burly burgrave
Who boasted he bold was and brave.
But he blushed, it is said,
Till his beard turned quite red,
So he thought it were better to shave.

C was a cook from Chang-Chew
Who once made a crocodile stew.
But when called by the bell,
His red pepper-box fell,
So that all he could answer was "Tchew."

D was a dignified dame
Who doubtless was not much to blame.
She played draughts with a lord,
And was dreadfully bored,
Which occasioned the loss of her game.

E was an exquisite elf
Who enjoyed being quite by herself.
She delighted to play
In an elegant way
With the things that she found on a shelf.

F was a fanciful frog
　Who stayed fifty years on a log;
　　For he never would spend
　　A night out with a friend,
As he feared to be lost in a fog.

G was a giddy young girl,
With a gaudy green hat and a curl.
She was not commonplace,
And displayed so much grace
While playing at golf with an earl.

H was a hard-headed hare
Who had such a horrible scare!
    As he opened one day,
    In the most heedless way,
A hamper marked "handle with care"!

I was an impudent imp
Who invited an over-cooked shrimp
  To a slide on the ice,
  As the weather was nice.
Next day the shrimp walked with a limp.

J was a juvenile Jap
Who met with a dreadful mishap;
For she bitterly cried,
When an insect she spied
On her flower, just taking a nap.

K was a kind-hearted King
Who once taught a bird how to sing,
  By knocking a pan
  With the knob of a fan,
And a kettle tied on to a string.

L was a Lorn little lass
With a grief that no grief could surpass.
John had left for the field
With his sword, lance, and shield,
And his luncheon inside his cuirass.

M was a merry milk-maid,
Who one morning was sadly dismayed;
For a mischievous mouse,
That Puss found in the house,
Was the cause of a slump in her trade.

N was a neat necromancer
Who once had a call from a dancer;
But he never let out
What she asked him about,
And a secret it made of his answer.

O was an obstinate owl
Who might have been quite a nice fowl;
But she spoilt her eye sight
Reading novels at night.
Now she ogles at you with a scowl.

P was a proud, pompous prince
Who lived on plum-pudding and quince.
Once he put by mistake
In his pipe a pancake,
And has been very pale ever since.

Q was a quaint dainty queen
Who once made a quilt for a dean,
    With some quadruple tweeds,
    Quite a number of beads,
And a queer little quill in between.

R was a rubicund rustic
Who wrote a romantic acrostic,
   In which roses and thrushes,
   And rabbits and rushes,
To the rhyme gave a flavour agrestic.

S was a short-sighted squire
Who solemnly sang in a choir;
And he passed from staccato
To a soft moderato
In a fashion that all did admire.

T was a tragical traitor
Who had more than one imitator.
    As he totally thrived
    On the gifts he derived
From the hands of the tender spectator.

U was a youthful Undine
In the kingdom of ultramarine.
Often week after week
She would play hide and seek,
In the weeds with an ugly sardine.

V was a virtuous vicar
Who played on the violin with vigour,
It was easy to see
The variation in C
Had not vainly been marked "a bit quicker."

What was the W then?
A whale, a wee worm, or a wren?
Or a witch of the wood
With a wonderful hood,
Who winked at a whimpering hen?

XZY

If there is anything to be said
In a verse about X, Y and Z,
Let us trust with the mission
This old mathematician,
Who carries them all in his head.